Intervening Early

Special Needs in Early Years Settings: A Guide for Practitioners
Collette Drifte
(ISBN 1-85346-856-8)

Early Learning Goals for Children with Special Needs: Learning Through Play
Collette Drifte
(ISBN 1-85346-936-X)

Handbook for Pre-School SEN Provision: The Code of Practice in Relation to the Early Years
Collette Drifte
(ISBN 1-85346-837-1)

Young Children and Classroom Behaviour: Needs, Perspectives and Strategies (2nd edn)
Sue Roffey and Terry O'Reirdan
(ISBN 1-85346-758-8)

Special Needs in the Early Years: Collaboration, Communication and Coordination (2nd edn)
Sue Roffey
(ISBN 1-85346-759-6)

Tried and Tested Strategies: Behaviour in the Early Years
Angela Glenn, Jacquie Cousins and Alicia Helps
(ISBN 1-84312-104-2)

Intervening Early

Promoting Positive Behaviour in Young Children

Nicky Hutchinson and Hilary Smith

 David Fulton Publishers

David Fulton Publishers Ltd
The Chiswick Centre, 414 Chiswick High Road, London W4 5TF

www.fultonpublishers.co.uk

First published in Great Britain in 2004 by David Fulton Publishers
10 9 8 7 6 5 4 3 2 1

Note: The right of Nicky Hutchinson and Hilary Smith to be identified as the authors of this work has been asserted by them in accordance with the Copyright, Designs and Patents Act 1988.

David Fulton Publishers is a division of Granada Learning Limited, part of Granada plc.

British Library Cataloguing in Publication Data
A catalogue record for this book is available from the British Library.

ISBN 1–84312–135–2

Typeset by FiSH Books, London
Printed and bound in Great Britain

Contents

Acknowledgements

This project began in 1999 as a collaborative venture between Bristol's Educational Psychology Service and the Behaviour Support Service. We wish to thank the original group – Liz Halson, Lesley Kaplan, Mary-Anne McCrystal, Zoë Stenner and Anne Gurner – for their contribution to the process of developing the assessment materials.

Thanks also to Joan Avery and Zoë Stenner for introducing the materials to schools as part of the pilot scheme, and to Jennie George and Elaine Davidson from the Learning Support Service for their contribution to the work.

We would like to give special thanks to Joan Avery, who gave much time and effort to the ideas for support in Part II of this book, and to our Administrative Assistant Karen Rogers for her never-ending patience and efficiency.

Finally, we are grateful to all the early years practitioners who have piloted this project and given us so much encouraging feedback.

Children live what they learn

If children live with criticism,
They learn to condemn

If children live with hostility,
They learn to fight

If children live with ridicule,
They learn to be shy

If children live with shame,
They learn to feel guilty

If children live with encouragement,
They learn confidence

If children live with praise,
They learn to appreciate

If children live with fairness,
They learn justice

If children live with security,
They learn to have faith

If children live with approval,
They learn to like themselves

If children live with acceptance and friendship,
They learn to find love in the world.

Dorothy Lawe Holt

Introduction

This book is the result of several years of experience supporting vulnerable children in schools and other early years settings throughout Bristol. It is in two parts. Part I is a screening schedule which identifies specific areas of concern for individual children's behaviour and Part II provides ideas, activities and strategies to enable practitioners to target their support effectively.

There are numerous books and articles about young people's behaviour which focus on school age children. This can be frustrating for those of us who work with the 3 to 5 age group, as we know that preventative work can be so effective at this early stage. Our aim was to produce a book which was clear and easy to use, and which focused specifically on the early years.

Many young children are entering early years settings lacking the basic skills needed to talk and play with other children. We can see, with depressing inevitability, that without effective intervention these problems will increase and the children may be caught in a downward spiral of social difficulties, disruption, disaffection and academic failure.

Research warns that if we fail to provide adequate intervention and support for our youngest children in difficulty, they will have a high probability of continuing to experience problems right through primary school and into adolescence. Adolescents showing serious disruptive problems often have a history of difficulties that began in the early years. Those whose antisocial behaviour began early have a significantly greater risk, both for chronic offending as adolescents and for careers as law-breaking adults. While the onset of delinquency occurs in adolescence, a wealth of research now indicates that the roots lie in early and middle childhood (Campbell 1995, Rutter 1993, Moffitt 1990, Webster-Stratton 1991). It is possible that with intervention in this age group we can prevent negative behaviours and reputations from turning into permanent patterns. At a recent international conference on adolescence, the Home Secretary, David Blunkett, stressed the importance of providing support for behaviour problems at the point where it can be most effective, namely from the moment a child enters nursery education (International Conference on Adolescence, 18 April 2002). It is increasingly recognised that the early years is the optimal time to begin preventative work with children in order to facilitate their social competence.

In Bristol Education Authority, we wanted to devise a systematic approach to early intervention and to provide structured 'catch-up' opportunities for children to develop emotional, social and behavioural skills.

Special needs teachers and educational psychologists worked together to produce a screening method for use in reception and infant classes in schools. This process involved referring to existing methods (e.g. The Boxall Profile), using a scoring system developed by a language specialist within the special needs service and pooling knowledge, ideas and experience.

As we have a particular interest in the early years, we modified the original screening method of ideas and activities specifically for the Foundation Stage.

This book is the culmination of four years of research and practice in Bristol schools and early years centres. It has evolved through our work with young children and practitioners in a variety of early years settings. While it is based on our own beliefs and practice, we are confident that it reflects the recent changes in early years education: the Foundation Stage curriculum and the development of early years partnerships.

When we first introduced our screening pack with resources, it was received with great enthusiasm as a practical and easy-to-use guide. Throughout the past four years we have been sharing these ideas with practitioners and evaluating their feedback, as well as reflecting on our own work. The materials have been regularly updated and developed as part of this process.

The screening and ideas for support are now used throughout Bristol and have also been introduced in other areas of the UK. Practitioners report that they are a valuable assessment tool with 'excellent statements for describing observable behaviours'. Many have found that they have provided them with a wealth of new ideas for supporting children.

The contents of this book should be relevant for all children in early years settings and can provide a useful framework for delivering the personal, social and emotional goals of the Foundation Stage curriculum. The book may also be used as an assessment tool or to provide information for outside agencies (e.g. educational psychologists).

In most early years settings there will be children who seem to respond to social demands differently from other children. Adults often find it disturbing that these children do not conform or participate in the way they would expect. Such children:

- never sit down in the 'welcome' circle,
- refuse to come to group time,
- are unable to play without hurting other children,
- run around uncontrollably without settling to anything,
- have frequent temper tantrums,
- are quiet and seem to have withdrawn into an unreachable world of their own.

As support teachers we are frequently asked to give advice on these children. In our approach we are as inclusive and positive as possible.

We feel concerned that children can become labelled as having 'emotional and behavioural difficulties' at this early stage and we prefer to look at a difficulty as a learning opportunity. For instance, some children may come into a setting already knowing the colour red, while

others have no idea what 'red' means. We do not label these children as having a difficulty; we accept it as our starting point as educators. In the same way, some children enter a setting able to play co-operatively while others do not seem to have a clue. We see this as a time to provide a range of opportunities, not a time to label or blame.

When a child's behaviour is causing concern, a natural reaction is to assume that the problems are within the child (professionals may seek ways to 'fix' the child). The approach we take in this book is to look at the whole setting, including the adults in it. In the strategies we suggest, we focus on the child's learning environment and look at different ways in which this can be adapted to introduce, teach and re-enforce social skills. We also emphasise the crucial role adults play in helping children to feel stimulated, recognised and emotionally secure.

To provide effective support for children, the adults also need to feel supported. Trusting relationships among the adults in an early years setting will help the children to feel secure. It is vital that every member of staff, whatever their role, feels recognised as a valued member of the team. Children's behaviour has a powerful emotional impact on adults and it is essential that this is acknowledged. Adults need to be able to turn to each other for support and advice without feeling judged. We hope that this book will encourage close working relationships between staff and a joint approach to helping the children in their care.

Equally, positive relationships between home and setting are crucial, and parents/carers need to feel acknowledged and listened to. In our visits to early years settings we are frequently impressed by the supportive and respectful partnerships between the early years setting and home. Most parents/carers are interested in the behaviour and well-being of their child and, when efforts are made to make the early years setting as welcoming and inclusive as possible, they become more actively involved in their child's emotional and social progress. We hope that the strategies and ideas discussed in this book will be shared with parents/carers and contribute to this process.

However, there will be some children for whom the strategies and suggestions offered here will not be sufficient. They will need further specialist assessment and support from other agencies such as health or social services. Practitioners have found the screening schedule (Part I of this book) useful for providing detailed evidence when referring a child for specialist help, since it categorises behaviour in clear and unambiguous language.

Finally, our hope is that this book reaffirms the good practice which we continually witness in early years settings. Many experienced and knowledgeable practitioners instinctively put good ideas into practice, and this book is an opportunity to share and celebrate their expertise and to recognise that, with the right support, the behaviour of our youngest citizens can change.

Nicky Hutchinson and Hilary Smith
September 2003

Throughout this book we refer to 'early years settings'; this term encompasses nursery schools, nursery and reception classes in infant and primary schools, early years centres, independent and voluntary sector nurseries as well as playgroups and registered childminders: in fact, any place where children between the ages of 3 and 5 are receiving care and education from qualified adults other than their parents.

PART I

Screening schedule

Using the Screening Schedule

Adults working in early years settings may use this screening schedule to help them identify children who are causing concern, and to focus on their specific needs.

The schedule consists of two parts:

■ **Whole group assessment** (page 3)
This should be completed for all the children in the setting after they have been attending for four to six weeks. By this time they should be more settled and adults will have greater knowledge of each individual.

■ **Individual assessment** (pages 4–9)
This describes aspects of each skill area in greater depth to enable the adult to assess the child's needs in more detail. It should be completed for children whose needs have been highlighted from the whole group assessment. Once completed, this assessment is designed to be used in conjunction with Part II, Ideas for support.

You may find it helpful to reassess individual children after 10 to 12 weeks of using interventions from Part II.

Whole group assessment

INSTRUCTIONS FOR USE

1. Please read the whole Schedule first in order to familiarise yourself with the categories.
2. In order to gain the most objective picture of the children, it is advisable to complete the assessment with a colleague.
3. Put an X in any column where, in your professional judgement in comparison with the 'average' child in your setting, you have concerns.

Setting: .... Completed by: ....

Date of Assessment:...

SKILL AREAS

Child's name	Emerging sense of self (personal and emotional development)	Self in relation to setting (response to the learning environment)	Feelings (ability to identify and express feelings appropriately)	Relationships with adults (interaction with adults)	Relationships with children (interaction with other children)

Individual assessment

Use this assessment for individual children whose needs have been highlighted from the whole group screening.

On a scale of 1 to 5, where:

1 = No concerns; 2 = Low levels of concern; 3 = Moderate levels of concern;

4 = High levels of concern; 5 = Extreme levels of concern

please rate the child's current skill level.

SETTING:.. GROUP: ....

CHILD'S NAME:.................................... DATE: ....

Emerging sense of self

	No concern			Extreme concern		Any additional notes

■ Appears to be open
and receptive

☐ ☐ ☐ ☐ ☐
1   2   3   4   5

■ Shows vitality and energy

☐ ☐ ☐ ☐ ☐
1   2   3   4   5

■ Is able to be calm and
relaxed at times

☐ ☐ ☐ ☐ ☐
1   2   3   4   5

■ Displays enjoyment
and sense of fun

☐ ☐ ☐ ☐ ☐
1   2   3   4   5

■ Shows care and
concern for self

☐ ☐ ☐ ☐ ☐
1   2   3   4   5

■ Can express likes
and dislikes

☐ ☐ ☐ ☐ ☐
1   2   3   4   5

■ Demonstrates a sense of
pride in own achievement

☐ ☐ ☐ ☐ ☐
1   2   3   4   5

Refer to Part II (pages 12–17) for ideas and activities

Self in relation to early years setting

	No concern				Extreme concern	Any additional notes
■ Follows daily routines	☐ 1	☐ 2	☐ 3	☐ 4	☐ 5	
■ Can cope with changes in the routine	☐ 1	☐ 2	☐ 3	☐ 4	☐ 5	
■ Shows curiosity and is keen to explore immediate environment	☐ 1	☐ 2	☐ 3	☐ 4	☐ 5	
■ Is willing/able to participate in a variety of activities	☐ 1	☐ 2	☐ 3	☐ 4	☐ 5	
■ Will attempt new skills/ activities	☐ 1	☐ 2	☐ 3	☐ 4	☐ 5	

■ Can focus on a task for increasing amounts of time:

(i) self-directed	☐ 1	☐ 2	☐ 3	☐ 4	☐ 5	
(ii) adult-directed	☐ 1	☐ 2	☐ 3	☐ 4	☐ 5	
■ Is willing to persist with a task even when it becomes challenging	☐ 1	☐ 2	☐ 3	☐ 4	☐ 5	
■ Shows a sense of belonging/ feels a part of their group	☐ 1	☐ 2	☐ 3	☐ 4	☐ 5	

■ Is able to:

(i) communicate simple choices	☐ 1	☐ 2	☐ 3	☐ 4	☐ 5	
(ii) follow through choice made	☐ 1	☐ 2	☐ 3	☐ 4	☐ 5	

Refer to Part II (pages 20–27) for ideas and activities

Feelings

	No concern				Extreme concern	Any additional notes

■ Is beginning to use words to describe own feelings (perhaps with adult prompt)

☐ ☐ ☐ ☐ ☐
1 2 3 4 5

■ Can identify how others in pictures and stories may be feeling

☐ ☐ ☐ ☐ ☐
1 2 3 4 5

■ Can recognise how others may be feeling in real situations

☐ ☐ ☐ ☐ ☐
1 2 3 4 5

■ Can reflect upon their own feelings after an event

☐ ☐ ☐ ☐ ☐
1 2 3 4 5

■ Is beginning to develop strategies for coping with strong feelings (e.g. can divert self away from temper tantrum)

☐ ☐ ☐ ☐ ☐
1 2 3 4 5

■ Can express affection

☐ ☐ ☐ ☐ ☐
1 2 3 4 5

Refer to Part II (pages 28–35) for ideas and activities

Relationships with adults

	No concern			Extreme concern	Any additional notes

- Can separate from main carer

  ☐ 1   ☐ 2   ☐ 3   ☐ 4   ☐ 5

- Has a positive relationship with at least one adult in the early years setting

  ☐ 1   ☐ 2   ☐ 3   ☐ 4   ☐ 5

- Is able to:

  (i)   express needs to an adult

  ☐ 1   ☐ 2   ☐ 3   ☐ 4   ☐ 5

  (ii)   initiate communication with an adult

  ☐ 1   ☐ 2   ☐ 3   ☐ 4   ☐ 5

  (iii)   respond to simple conversation

  ☐ 1   ☐ 2   ☐ 3   ☐ 4   ☐ 5

  (iv)   accept comfort/ reassurance from an adult

  ☐ 1   ☐ 2   ☐ 3   ☐ 4   ☐ 5

  (v)   participate in activities without direct adult support

  ☐ 1   ☐ 2   ☐ 3   ☐ 4   ☐ 5

- Is able to follow simple adult instructions:

  (i)   when given directly one-to-one

  ☐ 1   ☐ 2   ☐ 3   ☐ 4   ☐ 5

  (ii)   when given to the group

  ☐ 1   ☐ 2   ☐ 3   ☐ 4   ☐ 5

- Accepts adult's authority when necessary

  ☐ 1   ☐ 2   ☐ 3   ☐ 4   ☐ 5

- Shows a positive response to adult's praise

  ☐ 1   ☐ 2   ☐ 3   ☐ 4   ☐ 5

Refer to Part II (pages 36–41) for ideas and activities

Relationships with children

	No concern			Extreme concern		Any additional notes

- Is able to play alongside other children (parallel play)

  ☐1 ☐2 ☐3 ☐4 ☐5

- Appears to play co-operatively with other children:

  (i)　during adult-led activities

  ☐1 ☐2 ☐3 ☐4 ☐5

  (ii)　during less structured activities

  ☐1 ☐2 ☐3 ☐4 ☐5

- Will initiate communication with another child

  ☐1 ☐2 ☐3 ☐4 ☐5

- Is beginning to show concern for others

  ☐1 ☐2 ☐3 ☐4 ☐5

- Appears to be accepted by the peer group

  ☐1 ☐2 ☐3 ☐4 ☐5

- Is willing to share

  ☐1 ☐2 ☐3 ☐4 ☐5

- Is able to take turns:

  (i)　with adult supervision

  ☐1 ☐2 ☐3 ☐4 ☐5

  (ii)　without adult supervision

  ☐1 ☐2 ☐3 ☐4 ☐5

- Seeks help from an adult to resolve difficulty/conflict with another child

  ☐1 ☐2 ☐3 ☐4 ☐5

Refer to Part II (pages 42–47) for ideas and activities

PART II

Ideas for support

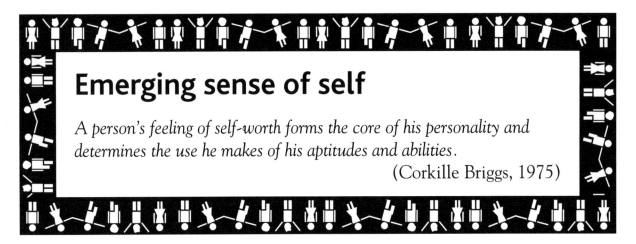

Emerging sense of self

A person's feeling of self-worth forms the core of his personality and determines the use he makes of his aptitudes and abilities.

(Corkille Briggs, 1975)

1 An adult's sense of self-worth has a direct influence on the way children value themselves. Ways to make your setting a positive and supportive place for adults might include:

- making the staffroom comfortable and welcoming,
- having treats such as a staff 'fun' day,
- greeting everyone each day,
- making time to listen to each other,
- setting aside time in meetings to celebrate good news and personal events, successes/achievements.

Develop and maintain a positive atmosphere in your setting so that both adults and children feel recognised, valued and supported.

2 Use a wide range of strategies for acknowledging all levels of effort and involvement. Ensure that your positive comments cover the full range of learning experiences. Acknowledge a child's efforts to help a friend as much as their efforts to produce a model.

Different children will respond to different approaches, so use as many strategies as you can. Some settings use rewards to encourage appropriate behaviours. If you choose to use rewards change them frequently to keep them fresh, and share ideas with colleagues. Here are some examples:

- Find ways to acknowledge the smallest of improvements/achievements. This could be as simple as a smile or a touch on the shoulder.
- In addition to acknowledging the efforts of individual children, recognise and praise group achievements to help foster a sense of belonging and 'group pride'.
- Ensure that each child is able to have at least one success every day. Give opportunities for children to show and tell each other about their achievements.

Individual rewards

Play game with adult

First out to play/dinner/home

Taking a message

Giving out milk/snacks

Stickers/stamps/star charts

Approaching another member of staff for special attention

Certificates/notes home

The Star today is **Darren**

Being star of the day

Choosing the group story/song/game

I listen carefully

Group rewards

Special playtime

Parachute games

Video

Group game, e.g. Sleeping Lions

Extra story time

Trip to local park

Themed picnic

Group party

3 Ensure success.

- Ensure that the desire to take part is more powerful than the fear of failure. Break down tasks into small manageable steps.
- A child who is very unsure may be helped by watching another group/child perform the activity first.

4 Devise ways of supporting children to cope with failure and mistakes.

- Re-frame mistakes as good opportunities for learning.
- Be open about the mistakes you make.
- See mistakes as an opportunity to problem-solve a better solution. Do this together with the child:

> e.g. 'How can we make this better? What can we do?'

5 Encourage the child to value his/her efforts.

- Store and display children's work with care.
- Talk about pictures/models before children take them home.
- Notice and point out steps of progress (e.g. when they first make a contribution to Circle Time).

6 Promote an atmosphere where the children value each other and appreciate each other's similarities and differences.

- Each child could take turns in having the 'All About Me' box. This is an attractively covered box which they take home and fill with their favourite things to bring back and discuss the rest of the group. (Parent/carer involvement in this is essential.)
- Share 'news'.
- Celebrate birthdays.

7 Encourage a sense of respect for the efforts of others.

- Children can be encouraged to show their appreciation of others' efforts by making positive comments (e.g. hold up a painting and ask the children to find three things they like about it). Remind them to be careful of others' work.
- Children can be encouraged to applaud someone who has tried hard, overcome difficulties, persevered.

8   Create opportunities for self-expression, such as through role-play, drawing, puppets, music, dance and so on. Ask open questions and allow silence and time for the child's response.

> e.g. 'How is Floppy feeling?'

9   Identify children with low self-esteem and give them special attention.

Here is Simon sitting at the table to eat his toast.

- Take photographs of individual children being kind/helpful/persistent and display them in a book or on a noticeboard. Use labels which acknowledge the child and describe the desirable behaviour.
- Make a 'celebration' tree (picture or model) where each leaf acknowledges individual children's achievements. Adults write each child's successes on a paper leaf and the children stick them on the tree.
- Make a 'kindness chain' where every kind act is recognised by adding a link to a paper chain which is hung across the room.

Additional ideas for children who need further help

- Find ways to notice the smallest of improvements/achievements.
- Use visual clues to help the child see when he or she has achieved even the smallest of steps as part of a longer task or activity (e.g. a sequence of pictures showing the order of steps in each activity).
- Give the child some choice but from a limited range.

> e.g. 'Would you like to play in the sand or draw a picture?'

- Some children find it hard to accept praise. They may destroy their work, or become angry and confused by the attention. In such cases, a better approach may be to show that you are pleased with the child through private acknowledgement, such as a non-verbal signal (e.g. thumbs up, or a sticker which is not displayed).

■ When praising a child with low self-esteem, use 'I' statements and describe clearly the behaviour you want to encourage.

> **e.g. 'I like the way you helped Ben tidy the bricks into the box. Well done!'**

■ Minimise the risk of failure by presenting tasks that are easy to achieve. Let children taste lots of success before introducing one new element which might be more challenging. Take the risk for or with them. Present it as something they may be able to do if they have a go. You can work alongside them, asking for their help.

■ Admit openly to how we, as adults, feel when we make a mistake and how we sometimes need to ask others for help. Encourage a fresh-start approach to tasks that have gone wrong. Recognise children's own strategies for coping with mistakes.

■ It can be helpful to take responsibility off a child's shoulders when he or she has made a mistake.

> **e.g. 'Oh, that was my fault for not explaining it properly.'**

■ Quit while you are winning. If the child is flagging, stop and complete the task another time.

■ Give a child who spoils other children's work plenty of space to work in.

■ Wherever possible, sit by the child to coach and encourage him or her through the task. Some children respond well to a timer. Send home daily feedback about the successes of the day.

■ Compile an 'All About Me' book. The child could work individually or with an adult to assemble photographs and drawings about themselves and their lives.

■ Compile a book of 'Things I can do', or 'I am good at...'. Sometimes it will be enough to focus on 'Things I like'.

■ Looking at their reflection in a mirror (with adult support) can help children to develop a sense of self and explore how faces can show different feelings.

■ Where he or she has a particular strength, provide opportunities for the child to demonstrate and support other children who are not as able in this area.

■ Provide regular opportunities for very active children to let off steam and release energy (e.g. running around outside or jumping up and down on the spot).

■ Provide regular opportunities for calm, peaceful activities (e.g. lying down listening to music in a 'comfort corner').

Case Study A Emerging sense of self

Scott and his twin brother clearly had very different personalities. While Jack seemed lively and confident, Scott appeared to be quiet and shy. Scott followed Jack around and copied whatever he did. At planning time, he always waited to see what Jack chose to do before he made his decision (which was usually the same activity). Scott also let Jack speak for him and rarely initiated any communication. He was constantly watchful for Jack and the only time he was seen to make a spontaneous action of his own was when another child pushed Jack over. Scott immediately pushed this child back.

The reception teacher was concerned that Scott was in his brother's shadow and believed that he needed support to develop a sense of self, independent of Jack.

As they did not want to separate the boys, the teachers thought of ways to ensure that they always treated them as unique individuals (e.g. always naming them rather than saying 'the twins', encouraging their mum to dress them in different clothes and making a point of acknowledging their different qualities). This was especially important for Scott, whose generally quiet and sensitive nature seemed to be holding him back.

When the boys were greeted in the morning during registration, their teacher began to say hello to Scott first, giving him a non-verbal signal (thumbs up) and time to respond, before greeting Jack. At planning time, she made sure she chose Scott before Jack and gave him a visual planning card, so that he could select from pictures of activities without having to speak. At first he just pointed at the pictures but gradually he began to use single words, and over time he also began to follow through his plan even when Jack chose something different.

At group time, the teacher encouraged Scott and Jack to sit next to different children (not just each other) and used mix-up games from circle time to help this. The teacher also included Scott in a regular small-group activity, practising sharing and turn-taking games to help him make connections with other children. She chose the same children each time for a number of sessions and Scott soon became friendly with a boy who was also quite quiet. Before long, the teacher noticed that Scott was occasionally taking the lead in the group and had stopped looking round to see where Jack was.

She also made a photo display of the children working and playing in different situations and groups, ensuring that there were examples of Scott with a number of other children. These were referred to often, and she used questions such as: 'Who can find...?', 'Where is...playing?' 'Who is playing with...?' etc. to help reinforce Scott's sense of belonging to the class group.

The school had a reward system of stickers and certificates, and Scott's teacher used this to praise him for being careful, thoughtful and considerate. He also earned 'leaves' on the class 'tree' for his kind behaviour, which went towards a class treat of a dinosaur party. This successfully gave Scott some status in the class and he began to gain a positive reputation for being kind and helpful.

Each child in the class also had a turn to bring in the 'All About Me' box which they filled with their favourite things from home and discussed with the rest of the class. Scott had his turn before Jack and his mum helped him to choose what to put in it. Although he found it hard to speak in front of everyone, Scott's teacher helped him to show what he had brought and he seemed proud and happy.

After about a term, Scott's confidence had significantly increased. He and Jack were still very close but Scott was beginning to speak in the circle, was planning independently of Jack and had formed friendships with other children.

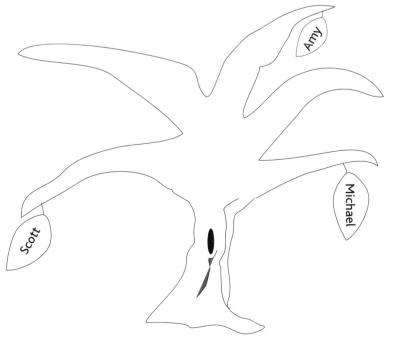

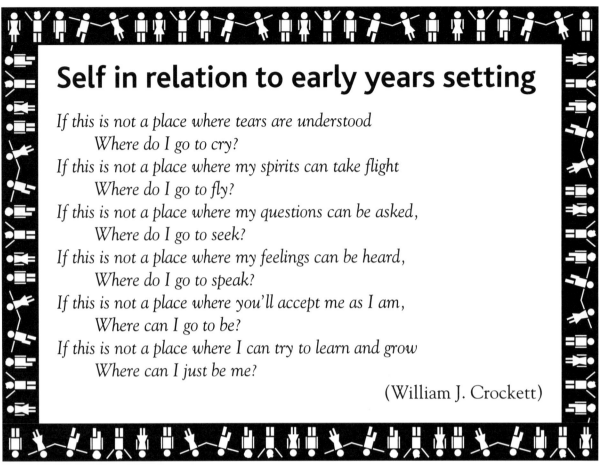

Self in relation to early years setting

If this is not a place where tears are understood
*   Where do I go to cry?*
If this is not a place where my spirits can take flight
*   Where do I go to fly?*
If this is not a place where my questions can be asked,
*   Where do I go to seek?*
If this is not a place where my feelings can be heard,
*   Where do I go to speak?*
If this is not a place where you'll accept me as I am,
*   Where can I go to be?*
If this is not a place where I can try to learn and grow
*   Where can I just be me?*

(William J. Crockett)

1   Make sure there is a clear structure to the day.

- Have some fixed times which may be used as reference points for the children.
- Present these times through pictograms/visual timetables, showing the order in which activities will happen.
- Use reminders and five-minute warnings when a change is about to occur.
- Provide opportunities for different social groupings within the daily structure.
- Have an entrance display to inform parents/carers of routines and special events. Make notices eye-catching, change them frequently and discard out-of-date information.

2   Anticipate the possibility of changes in the routine.

- Provide reassurance, explanation and support throughout these changes.

(e.g. 'I won't be here after lunch. Mrs May will be here to look after you.'

3   Ensure your day has pace and variety.

- Monitor the length of time children sit on the carpet. Don't make it too long. Certain children will find it physically uncomfortable to sit for long periods.
- Recognise that children's energy levels will drop if they are feeling hungry, tired or thirsty.
- Organise an indoor physical activity session if it is too cold or wet to go outside.

Monday

1.

| music | jigsaws | building blocks |

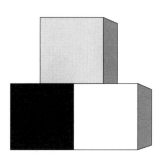

2.

| books | writing | painting |

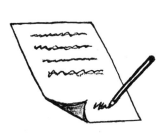

3.

| trike | sand | water |

Teddy bears party

Mums and dads, grans and grandads, please join us for our party on Wednesday 4th June at 2.00pm
Please bring a bear!

4 Create a calm atmosphere that is conducive to learning.

- Use a noise wheel/traffic lights to remind the children when the noise level is too high.
- Use soothing background music.
- Give children a vocabulary for understanding different levels of noise – quiet working voices, playtime voices, carpet-time voices, and build in regular practice times.

5 Have clear expectations about how the learning environment is managed.

- Ensure that children know what they can and cannot help themselves to. Use a colour code system:
  - red label = do not touch;
  - orange label = ask an adult first;
  - green label = help yourself.
- Make tidy-up time fun by using music, timers, reward stickers, singing.
- Set up clear routines and expectations for transition times (hand-washing, getting coats, going to lunch). When supervising these times, model and encourage patience, calmness and respect for others.

6   Use different ways to gain the children's attention:

  ■ If you need to speak loudly, reduce the volume once your point has been made.
  ■ Use visual signals (e.g. hands up in the air for the children to copy).
  ■ Use a chime bar or special bells.
  ■ Count to 5.
  ■ Sing a familiar song and encourage children to join in.

7   Foster a sense of belonging.

  ■ Develop rituals, particular times, songs and rhymes that are special to the group.
  ■ Use photographs to identify group members.
  ■ Use group praise and reward.
  ■ Provide occasions when different groups can show others what they have been doing.
  ■ Use circle time to provide an opportunity to develop group cohesion.

8   In this section we use the term 'rules'. Some practitioners are uneasy about the use of this word as they feel it may imply a system that is punitive or undemocratic. While we acknowledge these concerns it is important that children experience clear boundaries and guidelines for appropriate behaviours.

  ■ Develop as a team two or three rules which:
    – apply to every situation in your setting;
    – describe clear observable behaviours;
    – are age-appropriate;
    – are realistic;
    – are respectful and inclusive;
    – are worded positively (e.g. 'We are kind to each other.' 'We help each other.')
  ■ Teach and model the rules creatively:
    – display them attractively and at children's eye level;
      support all children's learning styles by having rules that are easily seen, written, accompanied by pictures and talked about regularly;
    – have photographs illustrating the children following the rules;
    – ensure parents/carers are informed of the rules;
    – use role-play and stories to show and practise how the rules work;
    – encourage the children to draw pictures which illustrate the rules;
    – model the rules by putting them into practice yourself;
    – use songs/chants to repeat the rules regularly.
  ■ Reinforce the rules:
    – acknowledge the children when they are following the rules;
    – use praise that is specific, describing the rule the child is following;
    – focus on one rule for a period of time, giving particular emphasis and recognition to the behaviours which demonstrate that rule.

Additional ideas for children who need further help

- Give the child small jobs and responsibilities.
- Use an individual reward system (colouring-in chart, stars, stickers) for following the rules and routines.
- Designate a special place for the child to sit at a table or on the carpet. Provide a carpet square or a chair, or a special cushion if the child finds this difficult.
- Use non-verbal signs to the child (a pat, nod, touch) as rule reminders.
- Set up timed activities using a kitchen timer or sand timer.
- Provide a visual timetable. Take photographs of the child working in different areas and assemble these into the daily sequence. He or she can have a timetable with a pointer to show where he or she is. (See case study on p.26)
- Make a book of photographs or pictures to assist the child in making choices, called 'What shall I do now?'
- Make velcro badges showing a range of activities for the child to choose from and wear while doing the activity (see Appendix 1).
- Limit choices to one of two activities suggested by the adult. You could use a choosing box with one or two items to represent the two different activities for the child to select. As the child becomes more confident you could increase the range of activities from which to choose.
- Find ways to avoid one child disrupting a whole group activity. He or she may respond to a special toy or object to hold, or a special box of activities placed slightly apart from the group.

Case study B   Self in relation to early years setting

Bronwen was an only child whose parents had learning and communication difficulties. Bronwen herself had very little language when she came to the Early Years Centre and seemed reluctant to communicate with anyone. Separating from her mum or dad was painful and difficult for her, she screamed and clung to whichever parent brought her when they tried to leave and it took a number of weeks before she was able to wave goodbye without any tears.

A member of staff (Meg) became Bronwen's 'key' adult and tried to help her access the normal routine, but Bronwen just wanted to sit on Meg's lap or wander about, looking around. She rarely joined in the songs or activities during the welcome circle and sat down with her group only when it was time for milk and fruit.

Bronwen did not play with the other children and, if they approached her, she either ignored them or wandered off. She would occasionally draw, if encouraged, and began to play with musical instruments, but she mostly seemed to be in a world of her own.

All the adults involved with Bronwen were extremely worried about her. The staff decided to make a visual timetable for Bronwen, using photographs to show different activities in the order that they occurred in the centre. These were stuck on a board with velcro and referred to immediately before and after an activity. Bronwen soon became engaged with this and liked to take the pictures off the board when an activity had ended.

At the welcome circle, Meg had Bronwen on her lap and held her hands, guiding them to clap to the songs. Bronwen enjoyed this and soon began to clap spontaneously to the songs although she still did not join in the singing. Meg then encouraged Bronwen to sit next to her rather than on her lap and gave her a special cushion to sit on. Initially, Bronwen resisted this but gradually she accepted it and would go and get the cushion herself as soon as she arrived in the nursery. Eventually, she sat next to the other children, and not only next to Meg.

Having her special cushion also helped Bronwen to stay in group time for longer periods and she began to choose from photographs of activities to plan what she wanted to do. An adult would then guide Bronwen to her chosen activity, which was usually the musical instruments. Bronwen began to communicate using the instruments, having sound 'conversations' with Meg. Gradually, the other children became involved and started to play music games with Bronwen.

The strategies which staff put in place helped Bronwen to be less isolated and more included in the centre, but it was clear that she was going to need further support if her communication and social skills were to continue to develop. Staff used the assessment given in this book to provide evidence of Bronwen's needs and rate of progress, before and after putting the strategies in place. This was submitted as part of Bronwen's statutory assessment, and she now has a statement of special educational needs and is making good progress in her reception class.

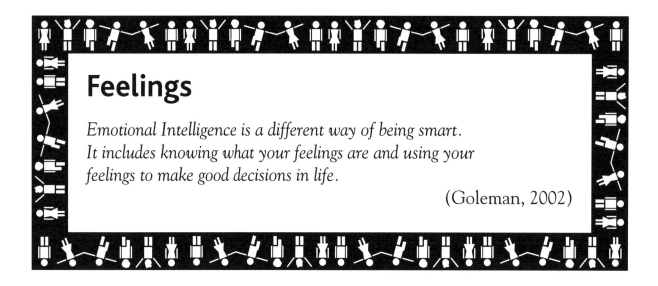

Feelings

Emotional Intelligence is a different way of being smart.
It includes knowing what your feelings are and using your
feelings to make good decisions in life.

(Goleman, 2002)

- Use every opportunity to talk about feelings.
- Provide vocabulary for feelings. Extend beyond happy and sad to worried, excited, frightened, puzzled and so on – supported by photographs, music, stories, puppets, role-play and modelling.
- Avoid trying to rescue the child from difficult feelings: stay with him or her and allow an open expression of feelings. You cannot always make things right and sometimes it is enough to listen and reflect on how the child feels.
- Reassure the child that it is OK to feel angry/sad/jealous, and explore appropriate ways of managing difficult feelings.

- Encourage expression of positive feelings too. Affirm times when the children are feeling happy/excited/proud. Artistic expression of feelings can be particularly powerful. Children can listen to happy, exciting music and make a collage expressing this mood.
- Make your own feelings poster, using photographs of the children/and or pictures of faces from magazines showing different facial expressions.
- Circle time provides an ideal opportunity for young children to explore and express feelings.
- Use sentence completion: 'I feel frightened when...'.
- Play games where the children have to guess the feeling state by reading facial expressions and body posture. Teach games such as musical statues where the children have to mime a particular feeling when the music stops.
- Model honesty about feelings by discussing with the children how you feel/being open about your own mistakes, apologising, asking children for their thoughts.
- Talk about how characters in stories might be feeling.
- Use 'emotions' puppets, posters and photographs to help the children identify different feelings.
- Encourage the children to respect each other's differences.
- Where appropriate, ask the children to be especially understanding towards a child who is feeling tired/unsettled/anxious.
- Model warmth and appreciation of each individual child.
- Make each individual feel he or she counts. Celebrate birthdays, special individual or family events. Have a special child/star of the day.
- Note if there are regular times in your early years setting when there is a higher level of problems (e.g. squabbling). Make changes to routines. Lower the emotional temperature by having a calm moment (listen to quiet music, light a candle).
- Some boys will have already absorbed the message that 'boys don't cry'. Support boys who are unwilling to show they are hurt or upset. Reassure them that it is all right to cry. Respect a need for privacy, guide them to a quiet place and wait with them until they have recovered.

Additional ideas for children who need further help

- Use adult support to interact one-to-one with children who need time to handle difficulties, or work with a small group, reinforcing work on feelings.
- Quiet and withdrawn children may respond to a gentle, non-verbal, undemanding approach. They need to feel they are visible and valued but not overwhelmed by unwanted attention.

- Understand that if a child laughs when being reprimanded it may be that he or she is having difficulty coping with feelings which need to be expressed. After the event, talk about appropriate responses.
- Children with communication difficulties may be in a state of extreme anxiety. Adults need to be particularly patient, understanding and supportive.
- Sometimes a child can be encouraged to talk about how he or she is feeling to a puppet or soft toy held by an adult, rather than addressing the adult directly.
- Some children have difficulties expressing feelings and do not or cannot approach adults. Help them acknowledge how they may be feeling (e.g. say, 'You've grazed your knee, I bet that hurts!' or 'I like that tower you've built, you must feel pleased with that!'
- Use stories and books on particular themes/events to help with specific traumas which you know a child is encountering (e.g. loss/separation/divorce).

Case study C Feelings

It was difficult to know what Sonia was feeling, since her face was always passive and neutral. She did not appear to smile or cry and seemed watchful of rather than playful with other children.

Her younger brother was born immediately before she began in the reception class and her mum was now pregnant again.

Although Sonia seemed to separate from her mum without any difficulty and quickly accepted the classroom routines, her teacher was concerned about her behaviour. Sonia began to hurt the other children without warning or provocation. Her teacher could not identify what triggered these incidents but they were happening several times a day to different children. When she spoke to Sonia after an incident, Sonia remained passive, giving no explanation and showing no remorse. She was asked to say 'Sorry' which she did mechanically and the incidents continued, Sonia sometimes biting or hitting but mostly pinching the other children.

The other children became wary of her and avoided being near her. Her mum admitted that Sonia had hurt her younger brother at home and she had to keep an eye on her.

The teacher thought it was likely that Sonia was feeling jealous and rejected. She discussed the idea of talking about feelings with Sonia's mum and encouraged her to do so with Sonia at home.

In school, she used Circle time as an opportunity to introduce the emotional curriculum to the whole class, using stories and photos of different situations to help the children recognise and name feelings.

She used mirrors to help the children practise showing different feelings on their faces and played 'guess the feeling' games. Sonia joined in with these activities and began to be able to name feelings, although she had difficulty expressing them herself.

Whenever Sonia hurt another child, the teacher would make it clear that it was not right to hurt others and gave lots of attention to the hurt child. She also used conflict-resolution techniques whenever appropriate, giving particular emphasis to how both children were feeling.

The teacher took photos of Sonia working and playing well with other children and made these into a book. She referred to this frequently with her, encouraging Sonia to recognise that she was being kind and friendly towards others in the photos. Sonia seemed to enjoy this book and often looked at it and showed it to other children.

The incidents of hurting gradually decreased, and Sonia began to relax and smile sometimes. She became more able to show her feelings through her facial expressions and, when asked, could say what she was feeling (from a limited range).

Before the new baby arrived, Sonia's teacher and her mum helped to prepare her. They shared books about 'having a new brother or sister' at home and school, and talked with Sonia about the different feelings it can provoke. When the baby was born, Sonia was encouraged to bring in photos to school and talk about him to the class. When he was a few weeks old, Sonia's mum brought him into school and it was Sonia's job to introduce him to the children. Her teacher helped Sonia to feel important and proud as the result of having a new brother, not diminished by it. It seemed to pay off, and there were no reported incidents of her hurting the baby.

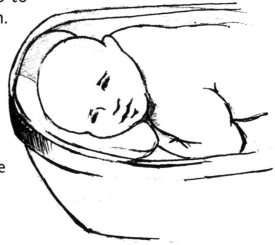

Managing angry outbursts

- A child who is feeling very angry needs a calm adult to stay with him or her. Young children should not be physically isolated.
- Other children may have to be removed and supervised elsewhere. This may be preferable to removing the angry child.
- Restraint must only be an option when:
  - there is risk of damage to the child;
  - there is risk of damage to other children;
  - there is risk of serious damage to property.
- Think about your body language when you are approaching an angry child. Adopt an open posture and position yourself at the child's level, alongside him or her rather than face-to-face.
- De-escalate the situation by talking calmly. At this heated stage there is no point in reasoning or discussing circumstances with the child. You might say, 'I will stay with you. I'm not going away.' Or it may be better to stay in silence with an occasional remark: 'It'll be OK/You'll feel better soon.'
- Explore triggers and consequences. Look for patterns and use the information to inform planning (e.g. Does the child always have a tantrum before going out to play?).
- It may be possible to divert an angry outburst with one of the following:
  - a special place (previously discussed with the child) where he or she can go to calm down;
  - a special box of calming activities that can be brought out;
  - breaking the mood by singing a song/looking at something special/listening for outside noises;
  - earphones with calming music;
  - a toy to hold or cuddle.

Find another adult who can offer the child a fresh approach.

- It can be distressing to be with a very angry child. It is helpful if other adults offer support to a colleague who has been managing a child's angry outburst. The colleague may need time out and the opportunity to talk about the effect it has had on them.

Case study D | Managing an angry outburst

When Isak joined the reception class, his teacher noticed that he seemed unhappy and sullen most of the time and rarely smiled. He followed the class routine and co-operated with her requests and instructions but seemed to do so reluctantly. His previous carers informed the school that they had found him quite difficult and he often had tantrums, but his mum told his new teacher that he was not like that at home.

Within a few days of Isak being at the school, there was an incident at dinner-time when he fell over in the playground and was hurt, but when an adult approached him to see if he was all right, he told her to go away. When other children tried to comfort him, he pushed them away too and went to sit on his own.

It was shortly after this incident that he had his first angry outburst in the classroom.

When the children were brought in after playtime, Isak refused to come in and, when he was guided in gently by an adult, he resisted and tried to run off, but the member of staff managed to get him into the class-room and lock the outside door. Isak became enraged and began hitting the glass door, shouting. He then threw himself down, hitting and kicking the floor, still shouting. The other children watched as Isak became increasingly distressed. His teacher approached him and he kicked out at her, so she withdrew and sent a message for assistance. By the time another adult had arrived Isak was sobbing, but as soon as the adult approached him he became enraged again and began hitting, kicking and shouting with renewed vigour.

Two adults lifted him up and carried him out of the room, and took him to the headteacher's office. He continued to struggle throughout, hurting both himself and the adults carrying him.

After ten minutes Isak was calmer, and was willing to be held and rocked by an adult. He sobbed in her arms for several minutes. When staff discussed the incident afterwards, they decided to prepare for the possibility of it happening again.

First, they considered what the trigger may have been and thought that it was connected to playtime. They put in place a number of strategies to help Isak have a more positive playtime, to encourage him to seek an adult or one of the school 'buddies' if he became hurt or upset and introduced a warning signal for reception children that the end of play-time was approaching. They also gave Isak the option of coming in five minutes before the end of play to have some one-to-one time with his teacher.

They decided that, if he did become enraged, they would first remove the other children to another room and an allocated adult would then come to sit with Isak. This adult would not attempt to touch him but would sit near him, saying calming phrases such as 'It's going to be all right' repeatedly and looking for signs that he was relaxing. When he was calm enough, the adult would take him to a quiet place and the other children could return to their classroom.

During the quiet time Isak would be encouraged to draw or look at books, but would be returned to the classroom as soon as the adult felt he was calm enough.

Talking about feeling angry and what is and is not all right and ways to express it, would happen at times when Isak was in a calm state, not immediately after an incident.

Isak did have another angry outburst and the staff put their strategies successfully into action. Isak calmed down much more quickly this time as no one tried to restrain or move him. The other children responded well, treating it as an emergency, like a fire alarm, but they did need time to talk about it afterwards. The teacher kept the discussion to anger generally rather than specifically about Isak.

As the relationship between Isak and his teacher developed, she found she was able to notice the early signs of him becoming angry and found ways to deflect it before he got into a rage. Discussions with Isak's mum also revealed other difficulties at home, and his teachers were able to suggest other agencies to support her.

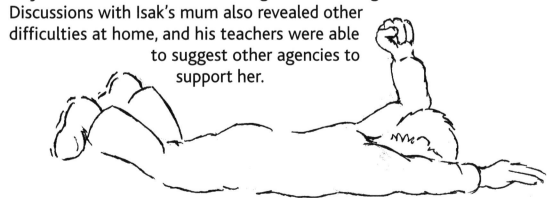

Relationships with adults

Ask anyone about their most significant experiences in learning and they will almost certainly start talking about the people who taught them.

(Salmon, 1988)

Ideas to support relationships with adults

Partnership with parents/carers

Children do best when all adults are working together in partnership. You can encourage this by:

- Supporting parents/carers and children during times of transition: home to early years setting, playgroup to nursery early years setting to reception class, reception class to Year 1.
- Take time to give a friendly greeting to children and their parents/carers at the beginning and end of each day.
- Make parents/carers feel welcome. Provide opportunities for them to become involved in activities.
- Invite parents/carers to special themed days and activities.
- Ensure that you give positive feedback to parents/carers each day about their child through stickers, certificates and comments.
- Use home visits to build a bridge between home and early years setting. Develop family support work if possible or appropriate.
- Make sure there is a notice-board to keep parents informed.
- Enlist parents' help with play activities and use their specialist skills.
- Provide opportunities for adult special interest groups if possible (e.g. first aid, keep fit, parent support groups.)

Adults in the early years setting

1 Children may encounter many different adults in the early years setting. Help children to accept and respond to adults whom they may not know.

- Introduce all adults. Use badges with pictorial symbols (e.g. a cartoon character) as well as their name.
- Display photos of regular personnel. Pictures and captions of staff made by the children can be displayed. Introduce adults on a daily basis, especially if they are new (e.g. supply teachers).
- Refer to adults by their name, repeating it frequently.

- Plan topics around 'people who help us'. Have adult visitors in.
- Allow the child time to adjust to changes of adult supervision. Prepare the child in advance: 'Soon you will be going outside with...'.
- Adults with responsibility for a group need to ensure that they spend one-to-one time with each individual every day.

2 When a child appears reluctant or unable to follow adult requests:

- Try to monitor when the difficult behaviours occur and identify what happens to trigger the behaviour. Find ways to pre-empt this trigger and help prepare the child for what is to come (e.g. for a child who runs away when it is time to come in after outdoor play, give him or her a job immediately prior to 'in' time (helping put away equipment, ringing the bells and so on).
- Some attention-seeking behaviours can be safely ignored, provided no child is put at risk. Give immediate positive attention as soon as the child does co-operate.
- Tell the child what you want him or her to do, not what you don't want (e.g. 'Tom, ask if you want the toy' instead of 'Don't snatch').
- Try to distract the child if he or she refuses to follow your request: draw his or her attention to something else, preferably something you can do together (e.g. 'Jo, look, there's the train...let's put the people in it' or 'Jo, I need your help with...'.
- Offer the child a choice of two activities, either of which you would be happy for him or her to do (e.g. 'Khalid, you can ask for the toy properly or play with this other one').
- Engage in a game of make-believe: pretend to be a giant, mouse, monster and so on (e.g. 'I'm a great big monster! Who's taken my things? I'm going to stamp my feet until he gives them back!').
- Turn it into a challenge (e.g. 'I bet you can't put it back before I count to five... one, two, three...' or 'I'm going to close my eyes and see if you can put it back before I get to five...one, two, three...').
- Use a treat which you know you (or the child's carer) can deliver (e.g. 'Chelsea, as soon as you've tidied away you can play outside/have a sticker/play in the sand').
- Say what you want the child to do; say 'thank you' in advance (to show that you expect it to be done), turn and walk away (e.g. 'Samia, I want you to pick that up, thank you...'), then turn and walk away. If she does not do as you ask, repeat the instruction. Then when she does, say, 'Well done, Samia! That's really helpful.'

Additional ideas for children who need further help

Work to develop a positive, non-judgemental relationship with the child.

- Have faith that time spent in being positive and giving a child individual attention will eventually improve your relationship with him or her.
- Additional home visits may be useful.
- Give the child frequent verbal and non-verbal signs to reassure him or her of your attention.

- Provide opportunities where you are alongside the child but not demanding any response or acknowledgement.
- Be patient; it takes some children considerable time to feel at ease outside the home environment.
- A transitional object (e.g. a favourite cuddly toy) can some-times ease the child's anxiety. Initially, the child may like to have the toy at all times. Gradually increase the amount of time when the toy is not directly with the child but is still within sight (e.g. 'Teddy might get paint on him. Let's put him up on this shelf where he can watch you'). Move on to putting the toy in a special place out of sight, to be collected when the child goes home. Eventually, the child may feel able to leave the toy at home.

- Separate the child from the behaviours. Make it clear that you still value the child although you do not want a particular behaviour to continue.
- Avoid negative labels.
- Convey to the child that you expect him or her to behave well. Have faith that he or she will meet your expectations.

- If you feel that you have 'had enough' of a child, get help, withdraw from the situation temporarily, or give your attention to another group.
- If you have had a particularly difficult incident with a child, debrief with a colleague and plan how you might deal with the same situation if it arises again. Record the incident and seek advice.

Case study E Relationships with adults

Jaspreet was a lively and popular girl in the nursery: alert, articulate and independent. She came from quite a large family and seemed to have no problems separating from her mum. She accessed the activities and equipment well and could play co-operatively with other children, although she tended to take the lead.

Difficulties arose whenever Jaspreet was asked to do something by an adult, particularly during tidy-up time. Sometimes she would run away from the adult or become 'engrossed' in something she was doing but increasingly she responded with a clear 'No!', becoming defiant and shrugging the adult away if they touched her or tried to guide her somewhere.

The situation developed to such an extent that Jaspreet was co-operating only on her terms and followed the nursery routine only if she chose to, often missing out on circle time and group time.

Her mum found her equally difficult at home, and adults at the nursery felt at a loss as to how to ensure that Jaspreet followed their requests and joined in more. They did not want to use a reward system since it did not fit in with their philosophy at the nursery, but everyone was feeling increasingly frustrated and concerned.

The staff decided to monitor Jaspreet's behaviour over a week to see if there was any pattern to whether or not she followed adult requests. It emerged that transition times were the most difficult: whenever there was a change of activity, Jaspreet was more likely to do what she wanted than follow the routine (e.g. refusing to join her group at Group time, or to stop playing and pack away at tidy-up time).

To help with this, the adults introduced a warning system to indicate that a change was coming up: a particular song was played on the tape-recorder. The children soon learned that the song signalled a change, and that when it ended the next activity would start. An adult always made sure Jaspreet noticed that the song had started, and it soon became her special job to put on the tape (which made it more likely that she would follow the routine).

In addition, at tidy-up time, Jaspreet was given a specific job to do, and staff found that by being explicit about it, rather than asking for general help, she was more likely to co-operate. She soon had her 'special' jobs and her mum began to give her one or two regular tasks at home as well.

When giving an instruction to Jaspreet, all the adults began to use a similar method: saying her name first, describing what they wanted her to do, thanking her, then turning away (e.g. 'Jaspreet, I want you to hang your apron up now, thank you'). This strategy proved to be quite successful, particularly when it was followed up with lots of positive acknowledgement when Jaspreet did follow the request, which began increasingly to happen. Staff also gave Jaspreet options, offering her some choice in what they wanted her to do. This way the adults still maintained control but Jaspreet felt she had some power. This was very effective in encouraging Jaspreet to come to group time. An adult might say, 'Jaspreet, do you want to sit next to me today or next to Sam?' or 'Jaspreet, do you want to go first or last when we do our review time?'

As she was quite independent, another successful strategy was to encourage Jaspreet to help others. Soon she became the one whom the other children approached for help with fastening their coat buttons or putting the drinking straw in their milk cartons.

Although Jaspreet continued to ignore some adult instructions, she became more likely to co-operate and stopped saying 'No' to staff. She began to join in Circle time and Group time regularly and became keen to do her special job at tidy-up time. Her mum was particularly pleased with the progress she made and said life at home seemed much calmer.

Relationships with children

Group relationships are vital in the birth, nurturing and maturing of self.

(Benson 1987)

1 Help each individual to feel valued.

- Make sure that all children know each other's names. Organise circle time games (e.g. clap the name, roll a ball to a named child, and songs which name the child).
- Encourage children to use each other's names.
- Greet each child by name as they enter and try to remember something personal to them.

> **e.g. 'Thomas, how's your new baby sister?'**

- Acknowledge all children through:
  - attractive name labels
  - self-portraits
  - photos on the wall
  - projects about 'myself'/'my home'/'my family'
  - birthday charts
  - news-board
  - celebration board (with personal news, such as 'Abiola has moved house').
- Use Circle time to give each individual the opportunity to share his or her thoughts and feelings in a safe and structured way.
- Choose a 'special person' for the day or week. Ensure that every child has a turn. The special person can have a particular chair or cushion to sit on, be first in the line, do specific jobs and so on. The child can be asked special 'getting to know you' questions by the rest of the group.

2 Give children opportunities to work with everyone else.

- In small group work, make sure that each child has the experience of working with every other child in the group.
- In Circle time use mix-up games (e.g. change places if you're wearing red) to avoid children always being partnered with the same child or children.

■ During outdoor play sessions encourage different social groupings. Make sure children circulate so that everybody has a chance to try different activities or play with other children.

3 Teach and reinforce the key social skills needed to get on with others; these include good listening, taking turns, making eye contact, being polite, using appropriate body language, saying sorry.

■ Role-play these skills using small-world figures (e.g. Playmobil), puppets, or the children themselves.
■ Adults need to model good social behaviour towards each other and the children at all times.
■ Make a display, using photographs and clear labelling, which illustrate these skills in action.
■ Enlist parents/carers to help with play activities and model these social skills.

4 Talk about playtime behaviour with the children.

■ Practise and teach playground games (e.g. 'Follow my leader', 'Duck, duck, goose').
■ Have a special 'cooling-off' place for anyone who is getting over-excited or too physical.

- Have a 'friendship stop', namely a place where children can wait if they have no one to play with. Get the children into the habit of including anyone waiting at the friendship stop.
- Mark colourful games on the ground (e.g. Hopscotch).
- Acknowledge and praise children when you see them playing well together.
- Join groups of children in their play when appropriate. (Adults can model co-operative skills.)

5 Plan ways to help children develop appropriate assertiveness skills.

- Discuss issues such as OK touching and not-OK touching. Reinforce children's rights to make choices and to say 'No'.
- Show them a clear gesture (e.g. raised hand) to go with a simple phrase such as 'Stop it', said firmly and with conviction. Role-play and discuss with all the children when this might be a useful strategy.

6 Teach ways to resolve problems and conflicts. You could use the following steps:

- Place yourself between the children, on their level. Using a calm voice say, 'You look really upset/angry/sad.'
- Ask, 'What's the problem?' and listen to each child.
- Re-state the problem by saying, 'So the problem is...'.
- Ask 'What can we do to solve this problem?' Encourage the children to think of solutions.
- Choose one solution together. Say, 'Well done! You solved the problem!'
- Be prepared to give follow-up support if necessary.

Additional ideas for children who need further help

- Observe the developmental level of these children's play. Do they play alone, alongside other children, or can they play with other children? Talk to parents/carers about their relationships outside of the early years setting. They may need patience and time to develop these skills. Identify the missing skills and target them.
- Use this information to provide opportunities for each child to experience play at his or her own level.
- When the child is choosing an activity, ask him or her who he or she would like to play with as well as what he or she wants to do. Then approach and ask the chosen child together.
- Set up opportunities to work with children who can be good role models.
- Rehearse with the children how they will respond to verbal and non-verbal signals given by other children.
- Teach them how to join in a play activity. Break down the task into small steps that the child can learn and practise (e.g. attracting attention appropriately, smiling, asking to join in, negotiating, and sometimes accepting a rejection).

■ Adopt a teaching framework of:

> Watch me
> Do it with me
> Do it while I watch you
> Do it alone

■ For a child who is not yet playing co-operatively with others, join him or her in parallel play and comment on what you or the child is doing. Try and let the child take the lead by avoiding directive comments or questions. Gradually encourage another child to join you both.

Case study F   Relationships with other children

When Tony began at the Nursery in September, he already had a reputation in the neighbourhood for being aggressive and difficult to manage. At first he seemed to settle well, and staff were impressed by his self-help skills and how articulate he was. However, by November Tony was displaying behaviour which was frightening and upsetting other children.

He mostly chose to play outside and always tried to be the first one out. He would rush to the climbing frame and stand on the platform, claiming it as his. He would roar at children who tried to approach, although sometimes he would allow one to join him as long as they did what he wanted. Other games included chasing children, again roaring at them, shouting 'I'm a monster!', which some children found exciting but which usually ended with someone becoming upset or hurt.

The Nursery staff always use conflict resolution techniques but whenever they tried to engage with Tony to help resolve a conflict he usually ran away in a temper, and, if later asked why he had hurt another child, he became angry again, at one stage hitting, kicking and swearing at his teacher.

The situation continued to escalate, with staff feeling increasingly frustrated and Tony's mum increasingly worried. The other children in the Nursery were feeling threatened and scared, and Tony became more angry and isolated.

To help Tony, the staff team decided to focus on 'being kind' in circle time and group time to help reinforce appropriate behaviours. They used stories and puppets to illustrate this, and Tony joined in well with the activities, volunteering some really positive suggestions. All the children were reminded of their ideas for being kind before work time, particularly if they were going outside to play.

Whenever the children were seen being kind to each other, an adult would go and acknowledge them immediately. Staff made a point of watching for any signs of Tony being kind, however brief or small the incident, and he quickly became interested in gaining this positive adult attention.

Staff also drew up a list of behaviours which were unacceptable and everyone was vigilant about using a 'stop' signal (particularly with

Tony), saying 'It's not all right to . . .' and then giving attention to the hurt child. For example, when Tony was roaring at another child, an adult would approach and say, 'Tony, it's not all right to roar at Jamie, it frightens him' and then give lots of attention to Jamie. Tony did not seem to be affected by this at first but staff noticed that gradually the roaring and monster games stopped.

Staff also continued to use conflict resolution and since Tony was reluctant to engage immediately after an incident, he was given time to cool off first. This proved to be an extremely effective strategy and as long as he was calm enough, Tony was soon quite skilled at talking about what the problem was and thinking of positive solutions. It also helped that staff stopped asking him why he had done what he had. He no longer felt blamed and could engage fully with the process.

It became apparent that Tony wanted to have friends to play with but did not know how to go about it, and he had got stuck in a pattern which seemed exciting but resulted in others being frightened and not wanting to play with him. By offering positive guidance and boundaries, the Nursery staff enabled him to learn the social skills he lacked. Within a few weeks, Tony was no longer possessive about the playground equipment and the other children were no longer frightened of him. He was a much happier and more popular little boy.

References

Bennathan, M. and Boxall, M. (1998) *The Boxall Profile: A Handbook for Teachers*.

Benson, J. (1987) *Working More Creatively with Groups*. London, Routledge.

Campbell, S. (1995) 'Behaviour problems in pre-school children: a review of recent research'. *Journal of Child Psychology & Psychiatry*, 36, 1, 113–49.

Corkille Briggs, D. (1975) in White, M. 'Magic circle'. *Times Educational Supplement*, 30 June 1990.

Goleman, D. (2002) in Haig, D. *Times Educational Supplement*, 21 June.

Moffitt, T. (1990) 'Juvenile delinquency and attention deficit disorder: boys' developmental trajectories from age 3 to age 15'. *Child Development*, 61, 893–910.

Rutter, M. (1991) 'Pathways from childhood to adult life: the role of schooling'. *Pastoral Care in Education*, 9, 3–10.

Salmon, P. (1988) *Psychology for Teachers: An Alternative Approach*. London, Hutchinson.

Webster-Stratton, C. (1991) 'Annotation: strategies for helping families with conduct-disordered children'. *Journal of Child Psychology & Psychiatry*, 32, 7, 1047–62.

Recommended resources

Children's books

Books by Joy Berry (1996) Scholastic:
Let's Talk About Saying No ISBN 0-590-62425-3
Let's Talk About Needing Attention ISBN 0-590-62424-5
Let's Talk About Being Helpful ISBN 0-590-62423-4

The Bad Tempered Ladybird (1977) Eric Carle
Puffin ISBN 0-14-05-398-6

Nothing But Trouble (1997) Gus Clarke
Anderson Press ISBN 0-86264-841-6

Pumpkin Soup (1998) Helen Cooper
Picture Corgi ISBN 0-552-54510-4

I'm Like You, You're Like Me (1998) Cindy Gainer
Free Spirit Publishing Inc. ISBN 1-57542-039-2

The Most Obedient Dog in the World (1993) Anita Jeram
Walker Books ISBN 0-7445-7247-9

Sometimes I Feel Like a Mouse (1992) Jeanne Modesitt
Scholastic ISBN 0-590-44836-6

Books by Brian Moses, Wayland Publishers:
I Feel Angry (1994) ISBN 0-7502-1403-1
I Feel Jealous (1994) ISBN 0-7502-0652-7
I Feel Frightened (1994) ISBN 0-7502-0654-3
I'm Bored (1997) ISBN 0-7502-2129-1
I'm Lonely (1997) ISBN 0-7502-2130-5

Temper Temper! (1999) Norman Silver
MacDonald ISBN 0-7500-2704-5

Mouse and Elephant (2000) An Vrombaut
Hodder Children's Books ISBN 0-340-74426-X-CHB

Books for adults

Relationships Ros Bayley and Lyn Broadbent
Harlequin ISBN 1-902239-16-4

Books by Margaret Collins (2001) Lucky Duck:
Because We're Worth It ISBN 1-873942-09-5
Circle Time for the Very Young ISBN 1-873942-53-2

Time to Talk Books 1 and 2 (1995) Jim Green
Collins Book 1 ISBN 0-00318-790-X; Book 2 ISBN 0-00318-791-8

A Positive Approach (1994) Frances James and Ken Brownsword
Belair Publications ISBN 0-947882-33-2

Here We Go Round (2001) Jenny Mosley and Helen Sonnet
Positive Press ISBN 0-530122-1-2

Face Your Feelings! (Book and cards) (1993) Lawrence E. Shapiro
Center for Applied Psychology, King of Prussia, PA.

Self-esteem Games (1998) B. Sher
John Wiley & Sons Inc. ISBN 0-471-18027-0

The Peaceful Classroom (1998) Charles A. Smith
Floris Books ISBN 0-86315-277-5

Talking is for Kids: Emotional Literacy for Infant School Children (1998)
Lucky Duck ISBN 1-873942-32-X

Appendix 1

Activity badges

Listening

Reading/book sharing

Painting

Drawing

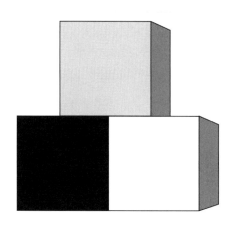

Construction toys

Play equipment

Tabletop activities

Water

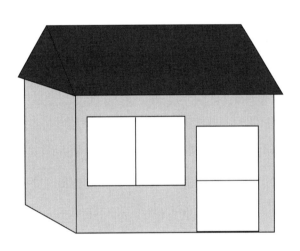

Home corner

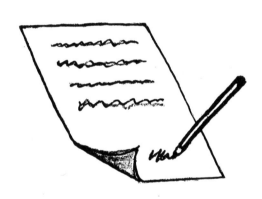

Writing

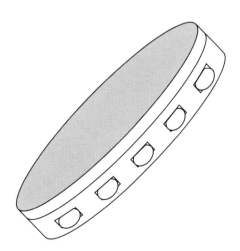

Music

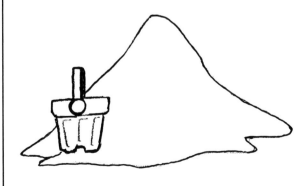

Sand

Appendix 2

Behaviour policy

Behaviour policy

All schools are required to devise a discipline policy and to promote good behaviour among pupils. Whilst this is not a legal requirement for all early years settings, there is increasing concern that the behaviour of young children is deteriorating and many settings are clarifying their responsibilities and outlining their approach through a behaviour policy.

At St Werburgh's Park Nursery School in Bristol, the whole staff engaged in devising a policy which reflected their aims and values as well as setting out the interventions they make when managing children's behaviour.

We have included their document here as we feel it is a good example of how to promote positive behaviour in young children.

We are very grateful to Sue Danvers and her staff for permission to use their policy but we must stress that it is unique to their setting and is the result of a long process including two training days led by Bristol Behaviour Support Service and several hours' work by staff at the nursery.

St Werburgh's Park Nursery School's Behaviour Policy

July 2003

Contents

1. Aims and values

2. Strategies to support our aims and values

3. Examples of behaviours and interventions

Aims and values

We believe that these are of equal importance and should apply to everyone.

RESPECT: to encourage all children to have respect for themselves, for other people (their feelings, beliefs and values) and for the school environment.

UNDERSTANDING & COMPASSION: to help children to understand other people's views and experiences and to be caring and tolerant of them.

RESPONSIBILITY: to enable children to have an increasing ability to take responsibility for their own actions and to understand the consequences of their behaviour.

FAIRNESS AND EQUALITY: to give children an understanding of how to be fair to all: how to share and give everyone an equal chance (within the context of everyone having different needs).

POLITENESS AND CONSIDERATION: to teach children how to be polite and considerate whilst acknowledging cultural traditions. In some cultures it is polite to make eye contact; in others it is not.

KINDNESS: to promote acts of kindness for each other and to assist children in ways of being gentle towards each other.

TRUST & SAFETY: to show children how to keep themselves and each other safe and to give them the confidence to express their concerns and fears in an appropriate way.

As a staff, we hope to promote these aims and values *through example* and hope that parents/carers using the school will join with us in partnership.

Strategies we use to support our aims and values

We help children look after themselves by:

- praising them: focusing on the positive things they do
- helping them to recognise their feelings and express themselves in an acceptable way
- encouraging them to ask for help from peers as well as adults
- encouraging their endeavours, identifying and planning for their interests
- building their independence through self-help skills
- encouraging them to see the good in others
- peer teaching (encouraging them to learn from each other)

We help children to care about others by:

- using conflict resolution
- modelling appropriate behaviour
- working on and reinforcing the understanding of feelings, e.g. in circle time
- naming and making feelings clear including the consequences of their actions: reflecting back to children
- being aware of the power of language, i.e. not being confrontational or negative
- boosting self-esteem
- giving time to listen and help aclnowledging their responses sensitively

We help children to be polite by:

- saying 'good morning' (we model the behaviour we want them to emulate)
- saying (and encouraging them to say) 'please' and 'thank you'
- encouraging them to wait their turn

- talking one at a time, listening to each other and not interrupting when someone is already speaking (all adults, including parents, as well as children)
- introducing new visitors at appropriate times and with sensitivity
- giving children clear messages

We ask children to look after equipment by:
- teaching them about health and safety
- encouraging them during tidy-up time: putting things away in the correct place
- encouraging them to help mend broken toys and equipment
- playing games, e.g. in circle time: putting toys in the middle and putting them away ('Where do they go?')
- having a group discussion in work time 'How do we look after this?'
- washing the bikes, dolls, Lego etc.
- reminding them to tell us about breakages
- having milk and apple at the table: no spills if possible!
- looking after the equipment ourselves, therefore modelling it

We help children to care about the environment by:
- making it as attractive as possible
- cleaning tables
- tidying up together
- displaying children's work
- tending the indoor and outdoor plants
- picking up rubbish
- making displays of interesting objects including natural materials
- providing labelled storage
- explaining proper care and use of areas (sand in the sand pit etc.)
- heightening awareness of plants etc. in the garden
- teaching about the natural environment
- modelling careful handling: noticing, acknowledging and praising positives
- sharing responsibility

Examples of behaviour

Children explore a variety of behaviours at this age. Most we consider ordinary, particularly when they are new to Nursery. Staff expect to deal with behaviour such as inappropriate shouting out, having a tantrum, snatching and walking away at tidy-up time etc. Intervention will be mild and may include one of the following:

- using a positive statement, e.g. 'If you want to throw something you could go into the garden and throw a ball'
- explaining our concerns, e.g. 'If you lean back on your chair you may fall over'
- giving them choices
- having a class discussion or circle time about acceptable/ unacceptable behaviours

Staff will deal with more serious misbehaviour by:

- labelling the behaviour not the child, e.g. saying, 'I don't like it when . . . ' or 'It's not okay to . . . '
- using non-confrontational language, e.g. 'When sand is thrown . . . ' Instead of 'When YOU throw sand . . . '
- using a short 'time out' on a chair or in another room
- informing the parent/carers

Supporting the child may involve setting up an Individual Education Plan (IEP) with specific targets related to behaviour (see Special Needs Policy)

Examples of behaviours which we consider extremely serious:
- racist remarks
- inappropriate touching
- biting other people
- threatening behaviours
- persistently hurting others

Our actions will reflect the severity of the incident but we will manage the behaviour without being blameful or punishing the child. Our intervention MAY include one or more of the following:
- removing the child from the situation
- when emotions have subsided, encouraging the child to face up to the hurt they have caused
- restraining or holding them if they are a danger to themselves or others (see below for physical interventions)
- seeking support from the head teacher
- in certain circumstances we may phone the parents/carers and request that they collect their child.

Serious incidents may result in a meeting with the head/teacher/parents to discuss the way forward. Occasionally, a shortened day may be more appropriate in order that the child's experience of school remains positive.

Physical interventions

On the rare occasions when we may need to restrain or move a child for their own safety or the safety of others, we will inform parents and ensure that we follow the guidelines and training we have received.

Parents and carers are an integral part of our school community. We will work closely with all our parents and carers in implementing our school's behaviour policy.

We aim to:

- share our expectations of behaviour at school during the settling in period
- talk to parents about any aspect of their child's behaviour which is causing concern
- be fair, non-judgemental and consistent in our dealing with behavioural issues at school
- offer support to parents and carers in managing their child's difficult behaviour by offering Parent-Line courses or getting advice from outside agencies

We expect parents to:

- communicate any significant changes in circumstances that may affect their child's behaviour in school, e.g. new baby, moving house, bereavement, divorce, separation and hospitalisation
- reinforce expected behaviour to their child by talking to him/her when at home
- support the nursery staff in implementing the school's behaviour policy

Appendix 3

Problem solving and conflict resolution

Problem solving and conflict resolution

In the section on relationships with children we offer advice on how to resolve problems and conflicts. Here is an outline of the steps as a reminder, with more detailed explanations of each stage.

It is taken from the High/Scope *Preschool Curriculum*. For further information contact: High/Scope Educational Research Foundation at *www.highscope.org*

We also recommend the following publication:
You Can't Come to My Birthday Party: Conflict resolution with young children (2002) by Betsy Evans, High/Scope Press ISBN 1-57379-159-8

Solving problems and resolving conflicts

1. Approach calmly

2. Acknowledge feelings

3. Gather information

4. Restate the problem

5. Ask for solutions and choose one together

6. Be prepared to give follow-up support

Steps for solving problems and resolving conflicts

1. **Approach calmly:** Observe as you approach, prepare yourself for a positive outcome. Be aware of your body language: it says a lot about your intentions and feelings. It is important to be neutral in order to respect all the points of view. If you do not feel able to stay neutral, use an 'I' statement ('I'm so angry because hitting hurts people.') and delay the problem-solving process until you are able to be neutral.

2. **Acknowledge feelings:** Give recognition to the feelings the children are expressing by using simple, descriptive words (you seem angry, sad, upset). Reflect the intensity of their expressions as well (you are very, very upset). This will help the children 'let go' of the feelings, perhaps resulting in a brief increase in their intensity, before their feelings subside. This 'emptying out' is important to do before the child can think clearly about solutions. Once this is done, let the children know you think that they can work out a way to solve their problem.

3. **Gather information:** Tell the children that you want to hear from each of them. Ask open-ended questions that help them describe the details of the actions or materials that are part of the problem (not 'Why did you do this?' or 'How do you think she feels?' – that's too abstract). Listen carefully for the details and needs; they are the key to finding the solution.

4. **Restate the problem:** Using the details and needs, as children have described them, restate the problem, clarifying any issues by asking for more detail, and reframing any hurtful language ('You can't play 'cause I hate you' can be reframed, 'You seem very angry and do you want to play on your own'). Check with the children if they agree that you have identified the problem.

5. **Ask for ideas for solutions and choose one together:** Respect and explore all the children's ideas, even if they seem unrealistic, considering how each might work. Help children think through the specifics of cause and effect so that complicated or general solutions become concrete and possible to do. Children may suggest, 'They can share.' This needs further exploration so that a set of actions that will happen is clear.

6. **Be prepared to give follow-up support:** Children may need help in implementing the solution, or difficulties may arise because one of the children is still carrying angry feelings that need further acknowledgement. Check with each of the children to see if the problem has been solved, especially children who have been very upset.

Appendix 4

Circle time

Circle time

Throughout this book we refer to circle time as a positive and inclusive practice which can be very helpful in supporting children's social and emotional learning. We have listed some titles in our Books for Adults which are specifically for early years and which follow the Jenny Mosley Quality Circle Time model. For further information visit the website at *www.circle-time.co.uk*.

Here we have included some guidance for setting up circle time in your setting and a series of six circle time sessions focusing specifically on feelings. They have been tried and tested in early years settings in Bristol as an introduction to emotional literacy.

The content was devised by Bristol Behaviour Support Service drawn from the experiences of practitioners in a number of early years settings. However, the circle time skills in Session One are taken from *Here We Go Round* by Jenny Mosley and Helen Sonnet.

Circle time – principles and practice

Principles

- Circle Time should be a safe, positive experience for all.
- Circle Time is inclusive, and all children can be helped to participate.
- Every child should be able to make an equal contribution during Circle Time.
- Adults are aiming to help the group become as self-directing as possible.
- Adults need to be mindful that these are the beginning stages of a long process. It will take years for children to develop all the skills needed. In the Foundation Stage, it is essential to introduce activities carefully, and be prepared to repeat them until well established. Progress may be slow, but the benefits will be enormous.

Practice

- Circle Time should be at a regular time, at least once a week – twice a week is best.
- Circle Time should be led by the same adult, with an extra adult helper joining in.
- The session should be quite short at first – ten minutes – building up gradually to twenty minutes, only if and when the children are ready.
- Each child has his/her own space marked by a chair, carpet square or cushion. Adults should sit at the same level as the children, that is, on the same size chair, or on the floor.
- Each child has a turn, even if she/he chooses to be silent.
- Adults should try not to pass comment on what a child says in the circle, other than to thank every child for contributing.
- If a child says something inappropriate in the circle, it is better to model appropriate responses, or remind him/her of the original prompt: for example, 'We were talking about things that make us happy', rather than dwell on the need to correct.

- If a child says unkind things to another, remind him/her of the need for everyone to feel safe and welcome in the circle.
- Some children will be unwilling to speak in this context, but should be encouraged to hold the talking object. They should be thanked for their participation.
- Some children will need more help than others, but it is not appropriate to exclude anyone. Strategies for managing potentially disruptive behaviour should be considered beforehand, and the least intrusive interventions made.
- Circle Time works best when a structure is followed.

Latest Publications for Foundation Stage Circle Time

Stepping Stones to Success – a two year Quality Circle Time programme for Early Years Helen Sonnet and Pat Child
Positive Press 2002   ISBN 0-9540585-0-X

Circle Time for the Very Young Margaret Collins
Lucy Duck Publishing 2001   ISBN 1-873942-53-2

Here We Go Round – Quality Circle Time for 3–5-year-olds Jenny Mosley and Helen Sonnet
Positive Press 2001   ISBN 0-9530122-1-2

Ring of Confidence – A Quality Circle Time Programme to Support Personal Safety for the Foundation Stage Penny Vine and Teresa Todd
Positive Press 2001   ISBN 0-9540585-1-8

Circle Time for Early Years Setting (Foundation Stage on FEELINGS)

Session 1 – introducing skills and rituals

1. Welcome & introduction to skills: 'in circle time we use our…

    eyes (to see)
    ears (to listen)
    mouth (to speak)
    head (to think)
    hands in lap (to concentrate)

2. Name Game: call out the name of the person next to you and pass the ball to them.

3. Mix-Up Game (Fruitbowl, using colours): give each child a small coloured circle of card (red/blue/yellow). When you call out their colour, they change places.

4. Sentence Completion – set out large different coloured cards to choose from

    – round (using talking object) 'I like the colour…,'

5. Ending Game: pass the bells

6. Thanks & reminder of 5 more sessions.

Session 2 – reinforcement

1. Welcome & skills reminder (see Session 1)

2. Name Game: call out the name of a person across the circle and roll the ball to them.

3. Mix-Up Game (Fruitbowl, using fruit!): give each child a small picture of a fruit (apple/orange/banana). When you call out their fruit, they change places.

4. Sentence Completion – set out a selection of real fruit to choose from

    – round (using talking object) 'I like to eat…,'

5. Ending Game: pass the smile

6. Thanks & reminder of 4 more sessions.

Circle Time for Early Years Setting (Foundation Stage on FEELINGS)

Session 3 – feeling happy

1. Welcome and skills reminder (see Session 1).
2. Name Game: song 'where is .... (name of child)? Sitting next to ... (name of child)' round the circle.
3. Mix-Up Game (Fruitbowl, using objects): give each child a small picture showing an object (ball/bike/book). When you call out their object, they change places.
4. Talkabout: show a picture (preferably a photo) of a child looking happy. Ask – what do you think this child is feeling?
   – how can you tell?
   – can you show me a happy face?
   – when do you feel happy?
5. Sentence Completion: set out a selection of pictures showing things that can make us feel happy (playing with a ball, riding a bike, reading a book etc.)
   – round (using talking object) 'I feel happy when... (choose one of the activities or make up one of your own)'
6. Ending Game: action song 'If you're happy and you know it... '
7. Thanks & reminder of 3 more sessions.

Session 4 – feeling sad

1. Welcome & skills reminder.
2. Name Game: each child takes it in turn to say 'Hello, I'm .... (say name)' and the rest of the group call 'Hello....... (name)'.
3. Mix-Up Game (Fruitbowl, using parts of the face): give each child a small picture of a part of the face (eyes/ears/mouth). When you call out their face part, they change places.
4. Talkabout: show a picture (preferably a photo) of a child looking sad. Ask – what do you think this child is feeling?
   – how can you tell?
   – can you show me a sad face?
   – when do you feel sad?
5. Sentence Completion – set out a selection of pictures showing things that can make us feel sad (being alone, falling down, waving goodbye to mum etc.)
   – round (using talking object) 'I feel sad when... (choose from the pictures or make up one of your own)'
6. Ending Game: action song 'head and shoulders, knees and toes'.
7. Thanks & reminder of 2 more sessions.

Circle Time for Early Years Setting (Foundation Stage on FEELINGS)

Session 5 – feeling angry

1. Welcome & skills reminder.
2. Name Game: each child calls out their name as they do a 'mexican wave' around the circle.
3. Mix-Up Game (Fruitbowl, using animals): give each child a small picture of an animal (dog/cat/mouse). When you make the sound of their animal, they change places.
4. Talkabout: show a picture (preferably a photo) of a child feeling angry. Ask 'What do you think this child is feeling?'
   – how can you tell?
   – can you show me an angry face?
   – when do you feel angry?
5. Sentence Completion: set out a selection of pictures of things that can make us feel angry (a child snatching a toy, an adult saying NO, a child not being able to reach something etc.)
   – round (using talking object) 'I feel angry when . . . (choose from the pictures or make up one of your own)'
6. Ending Game: copy a clapping rhythm.
7. Thanks & reminder of 1 more session.

Session 6 – happy, sad and angry

1. Welcome & skills reminder.
2. Name Game: choose a favourite from the previous sessions.
3. Mix-Up Game (Fruitbowl, using feelings): give each child a small picture with a feelings picture on it (happy/sad/angry). When you make a face showing the feeling they have, they change places.
4. Making faces: in pairs, children take it in turns to show a happy, sad or angry face to their partner, who then tries to guess which feeling it is.
5. Saying how you feel: give each child a picture from the selection used in the last 3 sentence completions (things that can make us feel happy, things that can make us feel sad, things that can make us feel angry). Ask each child, in turn to
   – look at the picture
   – show the feeling
   – say how they're feeling
6. Ending Game: choose a favourite from the previous sessions.
7. Thanks.